It is a **baby** elephant.

3

puppy

A **puppy** is a baby dog.

4

Read and Play

Baby Animals

by Jim Pipe

Aladdin/Watts
London • Sydney

baby

2

Here is a **baby**.

A mother feeds her **puppies**.

5

kitten

6

A **kitten** is a baby cat.

A **kitten** has soft fur.

7

piglet

A **piglet** is a baby pig.

8

These **piglets** are sleeping!

9

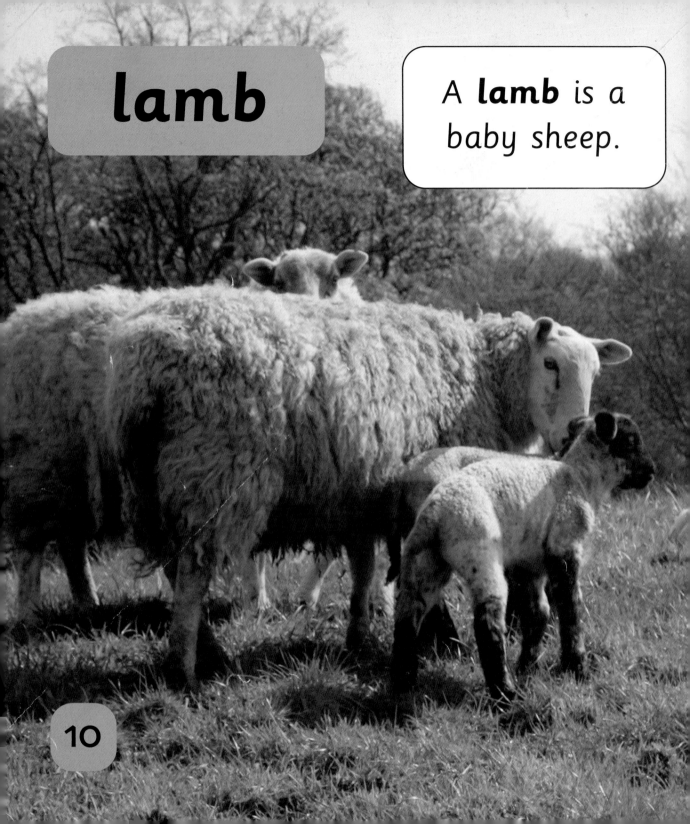

lamb

A **lamb** is a baby sheep.

10

A **lamb** has soft wool.

11

calf

A **calf** is a baby cow.

A **calf** is a big baby!

13

foal

14

A **foal** is a baby horse.

fawn

A **fawn** is a baby deer.

15

chick

16

A **chick** is a baby bird.

These **chicks** are in a nest.

cub

18

A **cub** is a baby lion.

A baby bear is
a **cub** too.

19

Who am I?

fawn

chick

foal

piglet

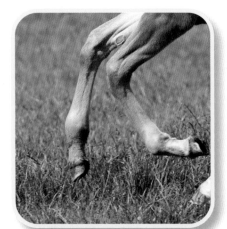
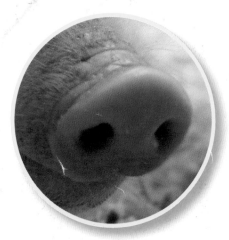

Match the words and pictures.

How many?

Can you count the piglets?

21

What noise?

Growl!

Woof!

Baa!

Cheep!

Make a sound like these animals!

Index

baby 2

calf 12
chick 16
cub 18

fawn 15

foal 14

kitten 6

lamb 10

piglet 8
puppy 4

Can you find these
baby animal pictures
in the book?

For Parents and Teachers

Questions you could ask:

p. 2 How are baby and adult animals different? Compare their size, shape and colour.

p. 5 How does a mother animal look after her baby? She feeds it, keeps it warm and safe.

p. 5 What do you think baby animals eat or drink? Mother's milk (mammals), worms etc (birds).

p. 9 Do you know the name of any animal homes? These pigs are living in a sty. Also stable, burrow, den, nest (see page 16).

p. 11 What baby animal would you like to stroke? Point out soft fur/wool on different baby animals. You could compare this with animals with scaly, prickly skins such as hedgehogs or crocodiles.

p. 13 What big animal babies can you think of? e.g. elephant, giraffe, hippo and whale calves.

p. 15 Why do you think a fawn has big ears and eyes? To see/hear predators/animal hunters.

p. 18 How do baby animals move about? Compare seal pup, bear cub, chick, foal etc.

p. 20 Who am I? If they need a clue, children can look back to pages 8, 14, 15 and 16.

Activities you could do:

• Ask the reader to act out what an adult animal does to look after its baby, e.g. feeding it, keeping it warm, clean and safe. Encourage animal noises!

• You could help the reader to build homes for babies, e.g. a sty for piglet made from straws.

• Encourage the reader to make a collage using materials that suggest animal skins. They could write labels: e.g. furry, scaly, smooth, hairy.

• Ask the reader to point out the body parts of different animals in the book, such as trunk, ears, tail, paws, claws and beak.

• You could talk about names for groups of animals, e.g. litter of puppies, herd, school, brood.

• Plan a special day for children to bring a "baby animal" stuffed toy to school. Encourage them to share information about their animals.

Paperback Edition 2009
© Aladdin Books Ltd 2006
Designed and produced by
Aladdin Books Ltd
PO Box 53987
London SW15 2SF

First published in 2006
by Franklin Watts
338 Euston Road
London NW1 3BH

Franklin Watts Australia
Level 17/207 Kent Street
Sydney NSW 2000

Franklin Watts is a division of Hachette Children's Books, an Hachette Livre company.
www.hachettelivre.co.uk

ISBN 978 0 7496 8975 9

A catalogue record for this book is available from the British Library.

Dewey Classification: 591.3' 9

Printed in Malaysia

Series consultant
Zoe Stillwell is an experienced Early Years teacher currently teaching at Pewley Down Infant School, Guildford.

Photocredits:
l-left, r-right, b-bottom, t-top, c-centre, m-middle
All photos from istockphoto.com except: 1 , 2-3, 6-7, 23tl , br & bl — Corbis. 5 — Comstock. 15 , 20br — Corel. 16-17, 20 tl, 22br — Stockbyte.

24